THE OFFICIAL MANCHESTER UNITED ANNUAL 2011

Written by Steve Bartram and Gemma Thompson

A Grange Publication

ISBN 978-1-907104-69-5

£7.99

Contents

Introduction

Hello and welcome to the 2011 Manchester United Annual. It's fair to say we enjoyed a mixed season last term. We were delighted to retain the Carling Cup, but fell just short in the Premier League and Champions League, where luck seemed to conspire against us at key times, not least when we were severely hindered by injuries.

I'm experienced enough to know you can't win them all. What you try to do is recover from every defeat and try to regain the upper hand next season. It's a challenge. We've faced challenges from clubs like Arsenal and Chelsea before, and each time we've managed to raise the bar at our football club - and that is exactly what we are going to do during the 2010/11 campaign.

But rather than tear the team apart and rebuild in a kneejerk fashion, I don't think there's any need to panic. In new signings Chris Smalling and Javier Hernandez, and Mame Biram Diouf who joined us last season, we have three players with great potential and whose futures are guaranteed for the club. Other young lads who come into that bracket are Kiko Macheda, Gabriel Obertan and Danny Welbeck, while Darron Gibson's starting to emerge very strongly and Jonny Evans has already proved himself to be a very accomplished defender. So we've got a good nucleus of young players and a good foundation to carry the club for a long time now.

Firstly, it is time to relive every twist and turn of last season's rollercoaster ride. Plus, in this year's edition of the Manchester United Annual, we hope you can learn a little more about the club's workings by going behind the scenes at our yearly awards bash and following our pre-season tour of the United States and Canada. And have some fun along the way, of course!

Sir Alex Ferguson

Season Review 2009/10

august '09

▶ **sun 9 Community Shield**
United 2-2 Chelsea
(Chelsea win 4-1 on penalties)

▶ **sun 16 Premier League**
United 1 Birmingham City 0
(Rooney)

▶ **wed 19 Premier League**
Burnley 1 United 0

▶ **sat 22 Premier League**
Wigan Athletic 0 United 5
(Rooney 2, Berbatov, Owen, Nani)

▶ **sat 29 Premier League**
United 2 Arsenal 1
(Rooney pen, Diaby OG)

John O'Shea kicks-off the players' recollections of the 2009/1 campaign, which opened with a mixed bag of results for th Reds...

"A lot had been made of us losing Ronaldo and Tevez during th summer, but the lads felt very confident going into the season We lost the Community Shield to Chelsea on penalties, but ther was no fear, just excitement about going for a fourth title in a rov We'd opened our last two league seasons with draws so we wer delighted to pick up three points against Birmingham. You don want to be playing catch-up, even after only one game. Captainin the side made it a very special day for me personally - I've done it i friendlies which is also nice, but to do it in a league game when really matters, for the manager to have that faith in me, is somethin I'll always cherish. We knew it would be a real battle at Burnley an unfortunately we just didn't produce on the night. It was a frea result, but we've always responded well to bad result with a great run of victories and it was nice to en the month with two good wins over Wigan an Arsenal. Wayne netted his 100th United goal i the Wigan victory – I think pre-season helpe him get the sharpness he needed and whe he has that he's hard to stop."

Owen v Wigan

Shortly after coming off the bench, the striker netted his maiden Reds strike with a typically accomplished finish in front of United's delighted travelling army. After latching onto Nani's lovely reverse pass, Owen clipped an unerring left-footed shot in off Kirkland's far post and grabbed United's fourth goal of the game.

stats

P	5	S	10
W	3	C	4
D	0	CLEAN SHEETS	
L	2	4	

LEAGUE TABLE @ 31 AUGUST 2009

Pos	Team	Played	GD	Points
1	Chelsea	4	8	12
2	Tottenham	4	7	12
3	United	4	6	9

september '09

▶ **sat 12 Premier League**
Tottenham Hotspur 1 United 3
(Giggs, Anderson, Rooney)

▶ **Tue 15 Champions League**
Besiktas 0 United 1
(Scholes)

▶ **sun 20 Premier League**
United 4 Manchester City 3
(Rooney, Fletcher 2, Owen)

▶ **wed 23 Carling Cup, Round 3**
United 1 Wolverhampton Wanderers 0
(Welbeck)

▶ **sat 26 Premier League**
Stoke City 0 United 2
(Berbatov, O'Shea)

▶ **wed 30 Champions League**
United 2 Wolfsburg 1
(Giggs, Carrick)

stats

P	6	S	13
W	6	C	5
D	0	CLEAN SHEETS	
L	0	3	

Owen v Manchester City

Arguably one of the most memorable strikes in United's history. Although the drama of the occasion catapulted Owen's winner into folklore, nobody should overlook the sublime skill involved in the goal's craft and finish. Giggs' perfectly-weighted pass rewarded Owen's intelligent movement, and the striker's sublime first touch and stabbed finish ensured a stunning end to a heart-stopping afternoon.

goal of the month

Six wins out of six ensured good progress in three competitions, but it was the dramatic derby win over City which was the undoubted highlight for **Patrice Evra**...

"After a really good performance and result at White Hart Lane, we kicked-off our Champions League campaign with a victory over Besiktas in Turkey. The defeat to Barcelona in the 2009 final was still very much on my mind before and after the game – we all felt we didn't give a true account of ourselves in Rome and were very determined to make up for what happened. Our next match against Manchester City turned out to be an amazing occasion for both the players and the fans. We could have killed the game off early on, but when we scored we started to make mistakes and sometimes you need mistakes to create a great game. It would have been very difficult to go into the dressing room if we had drawn - I think the manager would have given the hairdryer to everybody! To win in the final few seconds of the game was incredible. The players on the bench were running on the pitch, the fans, the atmosphere - this is why I say thanks to God I play in the Premier League and for United. After that we finished the month with tough wins over Wolves, Stoke and Wolfsburg and we were in good form all round."

LEAGUE TABLE @ 30 SEPTEMBER 2009

Pos	Team	Played	GD	Points
1	United	7	11	18
2	Chelsea	7	10	18
3	Liverpool	7	12	15

october '09

▶ **sat 03 Premier League**
United 2 Sunderland 2
(Berbatov, A Ferdinand OG)

▶ **sat 17 Premier League**
United 2 Bolton Wanderers 1
(Knight OG, Valencia)

▶ **wed 21 Champions League**
CSKA Moscow 0 United 1
(Valencia)

▶ **sun 25 Premier League**
Liverpool 2 United 0

▶ **tue 27 Carling Cup, Round 4**
Barnsley 0 United 2
(Welbeck, Owen)

▶ **sat 31 Premier League**
United 2 Blackburn Rovers 0
(Berbatov, Rooney)

Berbatov v Sunderland

goal of the month

With the Reds trailing 1-0 and struggling to get out of second gear, Berbatov galvanised team-mates and fans alike with a stunning scissor-kick equaliser. As United pressed forward, Sunderland only half-cleared as far as O'Shea whose right-wing cross was acrobatically fired home by Berba, who ended the month with a similarly spectacular finish against Blackburn.

stats

P	6	S	9
W	4	C	5
D	1	CLEAN SHEETS	
L	1	3	

LEAGUE TABLE @ 31 OCTOBER 2009

Pos	Team	Played	GD	Points
1	Chelsea	11	20	27
2	United	11	12	25
3	Arsenal	10	19	22

Positive results in the Champions League and Carling Cup for **Gary Neville** and his team-mates were tempered by dropped points against Sunderland and arch rivals Liverpool in the league...

"We went into October with great confidence following six straight wins. I think the international break at the start of September really helped us, we'd looked much healthier in terms of players training and playing more – I certainly felt better for getting more football under my belt - and our attacking flair was there for all to see. Unfortunately we kicked-off the month by dropping points against Sunderland, but Chelsea's defeat at Villa on the same day we beat Bolton got us back into a good position. Attentions soon switched to Europe as we returned to the scene of one of the greatest nights in the club's history to play CSKA Moscow at the Luzhniki Stadium. Despite a lot of injuries, we managed to get the win thanks to Antonio Valencia's first Champions League goal and his second in two games, but we suffered a setback at Liverpool, which is never a nice place to lose – especially because of the rivalry between the two clubs. We knew we had to pick ourselves up and move on, though, and we did that by winning against Barnsley and Blackburn."

november '09

- **tue 03** Champions League
  United 3 CSKA Moscow 3
  (Owen, Scholes, Valencia)

- **sun 08** Premier League
  Chelsea 1 United 0

- **sat 21** Premier League
  United 3 Everton 0
  (Fletcher, Carrick, Valencia)

- **wed 25** Champions League
  United 0 Besiktas 1

- **sat 28** Premier League
  Portsmouth 1 United 4
  (Rooney 3 - 2 pens, Giggs)

goal of the month

Fletcher v Everton

After Evra's cross was nodded down by Valencia into Fletcher's path on the edge of the area, the midfielder overcame the awkward height of the bouncing ball and thundered a sumptuous volley into the top corner, grazing Howard's right-hand post on the way in.

LEAGUE TABLE @ 30 NOVEMBER 2009

Pos	Team	Played	GD	Points
1	Chelsea	14	28	36
2	United	14	17	31
3	Tottenham	14	14	26

Despite controversially losing out to Chelsea at Stamford Bridge, Michael Owen says no-one was panicking inside the United dressing room...

"I was delighted to get my first Champions League goal for United in the 3-3 draw against CSKA Moscow. It was my second goal at Old Trafford and it came in a really entertaining game – they gave us a couple of scares but we managed to grab a draw in the end. The defeat at Chelsea was hard to take - there's no way on Earth we deserved to lose, but we walked away from Stamford Bridge with our heads held high and felt pretty happy with the way we played, and we showed our strength when we comfortably beat Everton after the international break. Although a young side lost out to Besitkas, we ended the month with a great victory at Portsmouth which included a hat-trick for Wayne and Giggsy's 100th Premier League goal. Even though we lay five points behind Chelsea we knew there was no need to panic. United usually hit top gear around Christmas and we were aiming for a long winning run."

stats

P	5	S	10
W	2	C	6
D	1	CLEAN SHEETS	
L	2		1

december '09

▶ **tue 01** **Carling Cup, Round 5**
United 2 Tottenham 0
(Gibson 2)

▶ **sat 05** **Premier League**
West Ham 0 United 4
(Scholes, Gibson, Valencia, Rooney)

▶ **tue 08** **Champions League**
Wolfsburg 1 United 3
(Owen 3)

▶ **sat 12** **Premier League**
United 0 Aston Villa 1

▶ **tue 15** **Premier League**
United 3 Wolverhampton Wanderers 0
(Rooney pen, Vidic, Valencia)

▶ **sat 19** **Premier League**
Fulham 3 United 0

▶ **sun 27** **Premier League**
Hull City 1 United 3
(Rooney, Dawson OG, Berbatov)

▶ **wed 30** **Premier League**
United 5 Wigan Athletic 0
(Rooney, Carrick, Rafael, Berbatov, Valencia)

With United decimated by defensive injuries, midfielder Darren Fletcher was forced into a spot of moonlighting in United's back four...

"We were pleased to get past Spurs in the Carling Cup fifth round and we followed that with a great display at Upton Park. Unfortunately, we picked up another defensive injury with Gary, who was playing in the centre of defence alongside Wes, going off before half-time. I was playing at right-back and Michael Carrick came on next to me to take Gary's place. The win in Wolfsburg was a real valiant effort from everybody. That was the first game in which we played a new formation with me, Michael and Patrice at the back and we just about managed to battle through it. The problem was, the longer we had to play there, the more chance there was of teams exploiting us. We lost against Villa when we didn't really perform, but Fulham was where we were found out. Craven Cottage is a tough place to go anyway, but to go with one fit defender, you know you'll be in for a hard time and they kept us under pressure throughout. Thankfully, we got a couple of defenders back for our last two games of 2009 and ended the year on a high at Old Trafford."

goal of the month

Gibson v West Ham

After netting two belters to secure a Carling Cup win over Tottenham just a few days earlier, Gibbo pulled another scorching finish out of the hat at Upton Park, thrashing home from 25 yards to complete a sublime counter-attack from the rampant Reds.

LEAGUE TABLE @ 31 DECEMBER 2009

Pos	Team	Played	GD	Points
1	Chelsea	20	29	45
2	United	20	27	43
3	Arsenal	19	30	41

january '10

stats

P	7	S	15
W	4	C	6
D	1	CLEAN SHEETS	
L	2		2

⊠ **sun 03** FA Cup, Round 3
United 0 Leeds United 1

⊠ **sat 09** Premier League
Birmingham City 1 United 1
(Dann OG)

⊠ **sat 16** Premier League
United 3 Burnley 0
(Berbatov, Rooney, Diouf)

⊠ **tue 19** Carling Cup Semi-final 1
Manchester City 2 United 1
(Giggs)

⊠ **sat 23** Premier League
United 4 Hull City 0
(Rooney 4)

⊠ **wed 27** Carling Cup Semi-final 2
United 3 Manchester City 1
(Scholes, Carrick, Rooney)

⊠ **sun 31** Premier League
Arsenal 1 United 3
(Nani, Rooney, Park)

As the New Year began, **Wes Brown** and his colleagues came up against some familiar foes, with mixed results...

"We made the worst possible start to 2010 by losing to Leeds in the FA Cup. It was a really tough defeat to take because it was a big occasion to play them again, and we just didn't perform. Looking back, we didn't want it as much as them. It's always disappointing to lose to your local rivals, but that day was especially hard to stomach. We then had a couple of hard-fought games against Birmingham and Burnley, from which we took four points, before it was another derby game against Manchester City, this time in the Carling Cup semi-finals. We played well and took the lead, but then got a bit sloppy briefly, conceded a couple of goals and somehow ended up losing a game we controlled for the most part. Wayne really started to come into his own from then on, scoring all four against Hull and then getting the winner in injury-time in the return leg against City – what a night that was. He scored again at Arsenal as we put in a terrific performance on the counter-attack and got three huge points. After such a bad start to January, that was the perfect way to end it."

goal of the month

Nani v Arsenal

The winger's wonderful effort missed out on the Goal of the Season voting because it was initially credited as an own-goal. It was retrospectively given to the Portuguese international, however - and deservedly so, after his outrageous skill, jinking run and cheeky chip over Manuel Almunia.

LEAGUE TABLE @ 31 JANUARY 2010

Pos	Team	Played	GD	Points
1	Chelsea	23	38	54
2	United	24	36	53
3	Arsenal	24	32	49

february '10

stats

P	6	S	15
W	4	C	7
D	1	CLEAN SHEETS	
L	1	2	

sat 06 Premier League
United 5 Portsmouth 0
(Rooney, Vanden Borre OG, Carrick Berbatov, Wilson OG)

wed 10 Premier League
Aston Villa 1 United 1
(Collins OG)

tue 16 Champions League, second round, 1st leg
AC Milan 2 United 3
(Scholes, Rooney 2)

sat 20 Premier League
Everton 3 United 1
(Berbatov)

tue 23 Premier League
United 3 West Ham 0
(Rooney 2, Owen)

sun 28 Carling Cup final
Aston Villa 1 United 2
(Owen, Rooney)

Berbatov v Portsmouth

The Bulgarian demonstrated his full array of talents with a marvellous fourth goal against struggling Pompey. Having expertly controlled a long ball, Berba meandered away from a string of challenges inside the area, worked his way outside the box and arrowed a superb low drive into the far corner.

goal of the month

Wayne Rooney was the undoubted star of a month in which United gained ground in the title race, and snared the season's first trophy...

"We started the month playing on the anniversary of the Munich air disaster, which is always a very emotional occasion. It was great to put five past Portsmouth that day, and I scored the first of a long run of headers. I'd worked on my heading and it was nice to see the rewards of that, but I didn't expect to score so many in succession – I ended up with six in March! We were a bit disappointed to draw at Villa Park, because we were the better team even though we had Nani sent off. Still, it was a brilliant feeling to go from there and win at AC Milan – they're such a great club and we'd never won in the San Siro before, and we played really well in the second half. The month was a bit of a rollercoaster because we then lost at Everton, which is never nice and I definitely get a bit of stick from the fans! It ended on a high note though because, after beating West Ham, we managed to retain the Carling Cup. Scoring the winner at Wembley is something you dream of as a kid, so it was great to do that."

LEAGUE TABLE @ 28 FEBRUARY 2010

Pos	Team	Played	GD	Points
1	Chelsea	28	39	61
2	United	28	42	60
3	Arsenal	28	35	58

march '10

As United's bid to bag the Premier League and Champions League gathered pace, Ji-sung Park took centre stage with some eye-catching displays...

"Traditionally, United get better as the season goes on, and that's what we did throughout March. It was a very hard-fought start to the month with victory at Wolves, thanks to another vital goal from Scholesy. Personally, my main remaining aim is to play in another Champions League final and win it, so it was a really good feeling to beat AC Milan and move into the quarter-finals – and it added to the occasion that I managed to score, of course! Wazza was fantastic against Milan again, and he kept scoring in the wins over Fulham and Liverpool too. People wondered how we would replace Ronaldo, but the way Wayne performed throughout the season helped us remain a great team. As for me, to score the winner against Liverpool, especially coming in front of the Stretford End, was an amazing feeling. Although we got another good result at Bolton in the Premier League, March ended in really disappointing fashion. To lose in the last minute to Bayern Munich, and to lose Wazza to injury, meant a good month ended badly for us."

sat 06 Premier League
Wolverhampton Wanderers 0 United 1
(Scholes)

wed 10 Champions League
second round, 2nd leg
United 4 AC Milan 0, agg 7-2
(Rooney 2, Park, Fletcher)

sun 14 Premier League
United 3 Fulham 0
(Rooney 2, Berbatov)

sun 21 Premier League
United 2 Liverpool 1
(Rooney, Park)

sat 27 Premier League
Bolton Wanderers 0 United 4
(Samuel OG, Berbatov 2, Gibson)

tue 30 Champions League
Quarter-final 1
Bayern Munich 2 United 1
(Rooney)

goal of the month

Park v Liverpool

If a player sheds blood to score a goal, he deserves recognition for it. Korean livewire Park took a hefty boot to the head from Glen Johnson in diving to head home Darren Fletcher's magnificent cross, but he barely noticed as he ran away to celebrate a vital, brilliant goal.

LEAGUE TABLE @ 31 MARCH 2010

Pos	Team	Played	GD	Points
1	United	32	51	72
2	Chelsea	32	53	71
3	Arsenal	32	40	68

stats

P	6	S	15
W	5	C	3
D	0	CLEAN SHEETS	
L	1	4	

13

april '10

sat 03
United 1 Chelsea 2
(Macheda)

wed 07
United 3 Bayern Munich 2, agg 4-4
(Gibson, Nani 2) – Bayern win on away goals

sun 11
Blackburn Rovers 0 United 0

sat 17
Manchester City 0 United 1
(Scholes)

sat 24
United 3 Tottenham Hotspur 1
(Nani, Giggs 2 pens)

stats

P	5	S	8
W	3	C	5
D	1	CLEAN SHEETS	
L	1	2	

goal of the month

Nani (1st) v Bayern Munich

The opening half of United's Champions League clash with the Germans at Old Trafford provided some of the Reds' best football of the season. Already a goal up, Nani impishly back-heeled home Antonio Valencia's cross to put United in charge. He then struck again, only for disaster to strike as Bayern hit back to go through on away goals.

LEAGUE TABLE @ 30 APRIL 2010

Pos	Team	Played	GD	Points
1	Chelsea	36	61	80
2	United	36	53	79
3	Arsenal	36	39	72

Stunned by the late defeat in Germany and the injury to Wayne Rooney, Paul Scholes and his colleagues endured a difficult April…

"It's always tough to come back from defeats like the one we suffered against Bayern Munich, and we started sluggishly against Chelsea and it cost us. We haven't had a good record in the Premier League after playing Champions League games anyway, but playing a fresh Chelsea side was difficult. We weren't great and decisions didn't go our way, but I thought we deserved a draw. To follow that by going out of the Champions League to Bayern was a real setback, and I think that showed in the way we struggled to create anything in the draw at Blackburn. After that came a really big Manchester derby. We knew we were up against it in the title race, but we also knew how important the game was to the fans. We played well, City didn't really threaten us and luckily we managed to get the win, thanks to one of the most important goals I've scored. Chelsea's defeat at Spurs later that day put us back in the hunt, and we showed our determination to press to the end with a really dogged, resilient win over Tottenham to end the month."

In his epic career, **Ryan Giggs** has witnessed some unlikely events during title run-ins, but he knew United were up against it going into May…

"Just before the Sunderland game we watched Chelsea go to Anfield and win really comfortably. That was demoralising, of course, because we know from experience what a difficult place Liverpool is to go to, but we still had a job to do at the Stadium of Light and I thought we were very professional in how we went about it. It's our own fault for letting our destiny be controlled by others in the first place, but we played really well at Sunderland, expressed ourselves and got a very good win. We all knew Chelsea were massive favourites to beat Wigan on the final day, but we still started the afternoon full of hope. We were doing our job against Stoke, were 2-0 up and then came in at half-time and found out Chelsea were 2-0 up and Wigan were down to 10 men. We knew then it was over and it hurt. We still went out and completed the win over Stoke, but it counted for nothing in the end because of the points we'd already dropped. The test now is how we bounce back, because we're all determined to be champions again."

goal of the month

Nani v Sunderland

The winger extended his eye-catching end to the season with a clinically-taken winner at the Stadium of Light. A neat, compact passing move culminated in the ball being slipped wide to Nani, and he expertly drilled in a low shot which swerved just inside Craig Gordon's far post.

▶▶ sun 02 **Premier League**
Sunderland 0 United 1
(Nani)

▶▶ sun 09 **Premier League**
United 4 Stoke City 0
(Fletcher, Giggs, Higginbotham OG, Park)

stats

P 2	S 5	
W 2	C 0	
D 0	CLEAN SHEETS	
L 0	2	

LEAGUE TABLE @ 09 MAY 2010

Pos	Team	Played	GD	Points
1	Chelsea	38	71	86
2	United	38	58	85
3	Arsenal	38	42	75

Celebrations

Player Profiles

Goalkeepers

1. Edwin Van der Sar

Born: 29 October 1970; Voorhout, Holland
Previous clubs: Ajax, Juventus, Fulham
Joined United: 1 June 2005
United debut: 9 August 2005 vs Debreceni (H), UEFA Champions League
International team: Holland (retired)
Best asset: The Dutchman's skill with the ball at his feet is unrivalled by any other goalkeeper in the game. United's accurate passing game is an unwritten club law, and having a custodian who can pick out a team-mate with either foot is an invaluable commodity, virtually giving the Reds an extra outfield player.

29. Tomasz Kuszczak

Born: 20 March 1982; Krosno Odrzanskie, Poland
Previous clubs: Hertha Berlin, West Bromwich Albion
Joined United: 10 August 2006
United debut: 17 September 2006 vs Arsenal (H), Premier League
International team: Poland
Best asset: An able deputy whenever called upon, the Polish international's stand-out quality is his shot-stopping. Coupled with his superb athleticism and agility between the sticks, he is a hard man to beat at point-blank range.

40. Ben Amos

Born: 10 April 1990; Macclesfield
Previous clubs: Trainee
Joined United: 1 July 2006
United debut: 23 September 2008 vs Middlesbrough (H), Carling Cup
International team: England (youth)
Best asset: For such a young goalkeeper, Amos displays tremendous awareness and control inside his penalty area. During his rise through the United ranks, Ben has demonstrated excellent handling and good organisational skills which, when added to his shot-stopping, makes a tremendous package.

Defenders

2. Gary Neville

Born: 18 February 1975; Bury

Previous clubs: Trainee

Joined United: 8 July 1991

United debut: 16 September 1992 vs Torpedo Moscow (H), UEFA Cup

International team: England

Best asset: Has there ever been a home-grown player with more passion and determination for the United cause than the current club captain? It's certainly hard to think of one in the modern era. Gary, the club's fifth highest ever appearance-maker, wears his heart on his sleeve every time he pulls on the jersey and shares an unbreakable bond with the fans who recognise he is one of them.

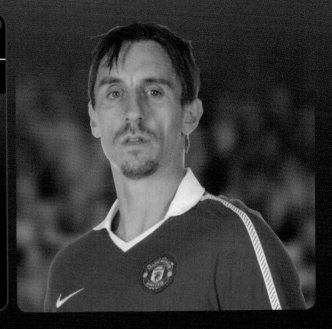

3. Patrice Evra

Born: 15 May 1981; Dakar, Senegal

Previous clubs: Masala, Monza, Monaco

Joined United: 10 January 2006

United debut: 14 January 2006 vs Manchester City (A), Premier League

International team: France

Best asset: There can be few players around who can match the Frenchman for fitness, speed and drive. Up and down the left flank with breathless abandon in every game he plays, Evra is the epitome of a modern full-back. He is a potent source of United's attacks, and a determined, rugged defender, making him arguably the world's best left-back.

5. Rio Ferdinand

Born: 7 November 1978; Peckham

Previous clubs: West Ham, Bournemouth (loan), Leeds United

Joined United: 22 July 2002

United debut: 27 August 2002 vs Zalaegerszeg (H), UEFA Champions League

International team: England

Best asset: Rio is calmness personified. Cool on the ball and composed no matter how big the occasion, he is also an astute reader of the game and a major influence in the dressing room. His leadership qualities have seen him skipper the Reds on numerous occasions, while Fabio Capello made him England captain in February 2010. Quite simply, one of the finest defenders in world football.

Player Profiles

6. Wes Brown

Born: 13 October 1979; Longsight
Previous clubs: Trainee
Joined United: 8 July 1996
United debut: 4 May 1998 vs Leeds (H), Premier League
International team: England
Best asset: The 'Longsight Libero', as he has been affectionately dubbed in some fans' circles since breaking into the United first team, remains an exceptional reader of the game. His ability to quickly deduce what an opponent is about to do next means few players manage to get past him.

15. Nemanja Vidic

Born: 21 October 1981; Uzice, Serbia
Previous clubs: Red Star Belgrade, Spartak Moscow
Joined United: 5 January 2006
United debut: 25 January 2006 vs Blackburn Rovers (H), League Cup
International team: Serbia
Best asset: A man who will put his body on the line for the United cause, Vida, as he is known to his teammates, has developed into one of the most imposing defenders around. The no-nonsense Serbian centre-back has also shown his qualities at the other end on the pitch, chipping in with a number of important goals.

20. Fabio da Silva

Born: 9 July 1990; Rio de Janeiro, Brazil
Previous club: Fluminense
Joined United: 1 July 2008
United debut: 24 January 2009 vs Tottenham Hotspur (H), FA Cup
International team: Brazil (youth)
Best asset: Just like his twin brother, Fabio is a bundle of energy and enthusiasm. A calm, considered defender, he also brings quality in attack and isn't afraid to get stuck in. Has already shown himself to be a more than able deputy for Patrice Evra, and can also slot seamlessly into the defence at right-back.

21. Rafael da Silva

Born: 9 July 1990; Rio de Janeiro, Brazil

Previous club: Fluminense

Joined United: 1 July 2008

United debut: 17 August 2008 vs Newcastle (H), Premier League

International team: Brazil (youth)

Best asset: The Brazilian's enthusiasm makes him exhausting just to watch. Hurtling into challenges, bombing forward in possession and generally racing about the field demonstrates his sheer love of the game, and suggests a bright, entertaining future at Old Trafford.

22. John O'Shea

Born: 30 April 1981; Waterford, Ireland

Previous clubs: Trainee

Joined United: 3 August 1998

United debut: 13 October 1999 vs Aston Villa (A), League Cup

International team: Republic of Ireland

Best asset: Players with the versatility of John O'Shea are few and far between. Having climbed through the United ranks as a centre-back, the lofty Irishman burst into the first team at left-back, and went on to start the 2009 Champions League final on the right flank. Having also enjoyed cameos in midfield and even in goal, Sheasy is a manager's dream.

23. Jonny Evans

Born: 2 January 1988; Belfast, Northern Ireland

Previous clubs: Trainee, Royal Antwerp (loan), Sunderland (loan)

Joined United: 1 July 2004

United debut: 26 September 2007 vs Coventry City (H), League Cup

International team: Northern Ireland

Best asset: Despite his tender years, Jonny has already shown he is capable of dealing with high pressure situations and top quality attackers. An unflappable and strong defender, the Academy graduate undoubtedly has a bright future ahead at Old Trafford as his manager has already testified.

Player Profiles

30. Ritchie De Laet

Born: 28 November 1988; Antwerp, Belgium
Previous clubs: Royal Antwerp, Stoke City
Joined United: 8 January 2009
United debut: 24 May 2009 vs Hull City (A), Premier League
International team: Belgium
Best asset: The young Belgian loves to get stuck into challenges and is a fine reader of the game, but it's his devastating pace which sets him apart from his peers. On the rare occasions an opponent can find a route past him, Ritchie merely switches on the afterburners and outruns them.

Midfielders

4. Owen Hargreaves

Born: 20 January 1981; Calgary, Canada
Previous club: Bayern Munich
Joined United: 1 July 2007
United debut: 19 August 2007 vs Manchester City (A), Premier League
International team: England
Best asset: His energy and endeavour have been sorely missed over the last two seasons. An all-action midfielder with vast experience, Hargreaves has the discipline to sit back and cover the back four and the power to push forward to add support in attack when needed.

8. Anderson

Born: 13 April 1988; Porto Alegre, Brazil
Previous clubs: Gremio, FC Porto
Joined United: 1 July 2007
United debut: 1 September 2007 vs Sunderland (H), Premier League
International team: Brazil
Best asset: Whether sitting deep or driving forward, the Brazilian's bursts of energy make him an invaluable defensive or attacking weapon. Having shone as a link between attack and midfield with his previous club Porto, Anderson has shown himself equally adept anywhere in the midfield minefield since coming to Old Trafford.

11. Ryan Giggs

Born: 29 November 1973; Cardiff, Wales

Previous clubs: Trainee

Joined United: 9 July 1990

United debut: 2 March 1991 vs Everton (H), First Division

International team: Wales (retired)

Best asset: Where do you start with the most decorated player in the history of the English game? Pace, skill, vision, an eye for goal and a set-piece specialist... the list is endless – Ryan pretty much has it all – as well as over 800 games under his belt as United's top appearance-maker. Arguably, the Reds' greatest ever servant.

13. Ji-sung Park

Born: 25 February 1981; Seoul, South Korea

Previous clubs: Kyoto Purple Sanga, PSV Eindhoven

Joined United: 8 July 2005

United debut: 9 August 2005 vs Debreceni (H), Champions League

International team: South Korea

Best asset: While Park is famed for his energy and incredible levels of stamina, which have established him as a firm fans' favourite, it's his natural intelligence and understanding of the game which makes him so unique. A dream for his team-mates to play alongside, his dedication to his role, selfless running and radar-slipping movement make him a nightmare for opponents.

16. Michael Carrick

Born: 28 July 1981; Wallsend

Previous clubs: West Ham, Swindon (loan), Birmingham (loan), Tottenham Hotspur

Joined United: 31 July 2006

United debut: 23 August 2006 vs Charlton Athletic (A), Premier League

International team: England

Best asset: An exceptional passer of the ball, be it long or short and with either foot. Michael is a cool customer in possession and has shown all the string-pulling capabilities in midfield which allow him to dictate the tempo of games.

Player Profiles

17. Nani

Born: 17 November 1986; Praia, Cape Verde

Previous club: Sporting Lisbon

Joined United: 1 July 2007

United debut: 5 August 2007 vs Chelsea (N), Community Shield

International team: Portugal

Best asset: Nani has been blessed with tremendous trickery, pace and power ever since arriving at Old Trafford, but consistently delivering an end product had been his downfall. Following Cristiano Ronaldo's departure, the Portuguese winger grew in stature, confidence and, most crucially, consistency to finally realise his brimming potential.

18. Paul Scholes

Born: 16 November 1974; Salford

Previous clubs: Trainee

Joined United: 8 July 1991

United debut: 21 September 1994 v Port Vale (A), League Cup

International team: England (retired)

Best asset: Paul Scholes giving the ball away is a rare sight in football. During his epic United career, Scholes has become a model of ball retention, invariably finding his team-mates, wherever they are on the field. Throw in his knack for being in the right place at the right time to bag vital goals, and it's little wonder that countless former colleagues regard Scholes as the best player they have played with.

24. Darren Fletcher

Born: 1 February 1984; Edinburgh, Scotland

Previous clubs: Trainee

Joined United: 3 July 2000

United debut: 12 March 2003 vs FC Basel (H), Champions League

International team: Scotland

Best asset: Energy. The Scot sometimes appears omnipresent, so vigorous is his approach to the midfield. Previously seen as a big game player, Fletch's consistency and high-octane contribution against all opponents in recent seasons has marked his evolution into one of the most complete midfielders in the game.

25. Antonio Valencia

Born: 4 August 1985; Lago Agrio, Ecuador

Previous clubs: El Nacional, Villarreal, Wigan

Joined United: 30 June 2009

United debut: 9 August 2009 v Chelsea (N), Community Shield

International team: Ecuador

Best asset: Wayne Rooney summed it up best: "When the delivery into the box is good you can work on your movement and timing, and I've benefited from Antonio's great work." Not only does the Ecuadorian winger possess the ability to beat a man from a standing start, his array and accuracy of crossing make him a striker's dream.

26. Gabriel Obertan

Born: 26 February 1989; Pantin, France

Previous club: Girondins de Bordeaux

Joined United: 8 July 2009

United debut: 27 October 2009 vs Barnsley (A), Carling Cup

International team: France (youth)

Best asset: There are few faster players around. Obertan possesses incredible speed over short and long distances. Allied to his impressive array of trickery, his fast feet make him a defender's nightmare.

28. Darron Gibson

Born: 25 October 1987; Derry, Northern Ireland

Previous clubs: Trainee, Royal Antwerp (loan), Wolves (loan)

Joined United: 1 July 2004

United debut: 26 October 2005 vs Barnet (H), League Cup

International team: Republic of Ireland

Best asset: A powerful midfielder who packs a powerful shot, few can strike a ball as sweetly as Gibbo. His passing range continues to improve, but it's his ferocious shooting which remains his biggest weapon, prompting United fans to bellow 'shoot' whenever he gains possession anywhere near the opposition's goal.

Player Profiles

Forwards

7. Michael Owen

Born: 14 December 1979; Chester

Previous clubs: Liverpool, Real Madrid, Newcastle United

Joined United: 3 July 2009

United debut: 9 August 2009 vs Chelsea (N), Community Shield

International team: England

Best asset: Prowess inside the opposition area. A few eyebrows were raised when Owen's arrival on a free transfer was announced, but Sir Alex knew he was signing a poacher with pedigree. For control and a cool head in front of goal, there are very few who could ever match United's no.7.

9. Dimitar Berbatov

Born: 30 January 1981; Blagoevgrad, Bulgaria

Previous clubs: CSKA Sofia, Bayer Leverkusen, Tottenham

Joined United: 1 September 2008

United debut: 13 September 2008 vs Liverpool (A), Premier League

International team: Bulgaria (retired)

Best asset: Berba's close control and use of the ball is second to none. An elegant orchestrator of the forward line, the unflappable Bulgarian has the vision and the skill to link play, as well as chip in with a goal or two himself.

10. Wayne Rooney

Born: 24 October 1985; Liverpool

Previous club: Everton

Joined United: 31 August 2004

United debut: 28 September 2004 vs Fenerbahce (H), Champions League

International team: England

Best attribute: Everything. It's hard to find a facet of Rooney's game which falls below the very top level. His natural talent prompted Sir Alex to part with a world record fee for a teenager in 2004, but Rooney has refined his game throughout his Reds career, and is now one of the most complete players in the world. United's heart, soul and goals.

19. Danny Welbeck

Born: 26 November 1990; Manchester

Previous clubs: Trainee

Joined United: 1 July 2007

United debut: 23 September 2008 vs Middlesbrough (H), League Cup

International team: England (youth)

Best asset: A natural-born entertainer, Danny is blessed with terrific trickery which has shone all through his rise up the United ladder. There are still lessons to be learnt for the Manchester-born striker, who can also assert himself on either wing, but the future looks bright.

27. Federico Macheda

Born: 22 August 1991; Rome, Italy

Previous club: Lazio

Joined United: 1 September 2007

United debut: 5 April 2009 vs Aston Villa (H), Premier League

International team: Italy (youth)

Best asset: Kiko boasts the brain and physique of a far more experienced player. A deadly finisher anywhere inside the area, the Italian also has a battling edge to his game and the upper body strength to give opposing defenders a torrid time.

32. Mame Biram Diouf

Born: 16 December 1987; Dakar, Senegal

Previous clubs: Diaraf, Molde FK

Joined United: 30 July 2009

United debut: 9 January 2010 v Birmingham (A), Premier League

International team: Senegal

Best asset: Allied to his pace and power, it's the striker's infectious enthusiasm which has really caught the eye. Off the pitch he is a real character, while he has already shown his willingness to work hard for the team on it. He can execute a pretty nifty back flip as well!

Sir Alex Ferguson always has one eye on the future, which is why he swooped to add these promising young talents to his squad during 2009/10, in readiness for the new season...

Name: Chris Smalling
Position: Defender
Born: 22/11/1989
Previous clubs: Maidstone United, Fulham

Chris Smalling's rise to prominence has been breathtaking. The towering young defender made only a dozen appearances for non-league side Maidstone United before joining Fulham in the summer of 2008. It took him under a year to make his Cottagers debut, still aged only 19, and he had made just eight appearances for Roy Hodgson's side before he agreed a move to Old Trafford.

By then, Smalling had been capped at England under-21 level and, as was the case with Chicharito, United moved to make the signing before he was snapped up by a rival club.

"We'd been watching him for a while," says chief executive David Gill. "We spoke to Fulham in January and told them we were very happy for him to continue on loan there for the rest of the season, hopefully playing some games and gaining experience around the first team, and then we would acquire him in the summer. There had been a lot of interest in him – Arsenal were particularly keen - so we had to beat off competition from them. We agreed a fee quite quickly with Fulham, we met with Chris and his representative and it went from there."

Smalling made a further 10 appearances for the Cottagers during the course of 2009/10, and his Fulham team-mate Danny Murphy feels United have snapped up a star in the making.

"Chris is potentially a wonderful player," says the former Liverpool midfielder. "He has great pace, is calm on the ball and good in the air. What more do you need from a good centre-half? He'll be a great signing for United and he won't look out of place."

Such an endorsement will come as no surprise to Sir Alex, who is well aware of the youngster's brimming talent. "Chris is an extremely talented young defender," he said. "He's a very good passer of the ball, quick and reads the game well. He still needs to develop his upper body physique, but that will come. He will be a great asset to the club, playing alongside some of the best defenders around. He's like a young Rio Ferdinand and I'm sure he'll do really well for us."

"Chris is like a young Rio Ferdinand – he's a very good passer of the ball, quick and reads the game well. He will be a great asset to the club."
– Sir Alex Ferguson

Name: Javier Hernandez (Chicharito)
Position: Striker
Born: 01/06/1988
Previous clubs: Club Deportivo Guadalajara

The day after United's Champions League exit to Bayern Munich, the club made the shock announcement that Javier 'Chicharito' Hernandez would be joining ahead of the 2010/11 season. An almost total unknown to most United supporters, the diminutive attacker is the club's first ever Mexican player, and is the third generation of his family to have represented Mexico at a World Cup. Javier's nickname, 'Chicharito', means 'little pea'. His father was known as 'Chicaro' or 'pea' because of his green eyes.

"It's a dream and I feel so happy," he said. "The stadium, the atmosphere at the club and the history are incredible and I want to do great things here. In our country Manchester United are the top team and all my impressions of the team, the club and the city are incredible."

"We watched him in a few games and we thought we'd just wait because he was only young, but then he came into the national team and we knew we were in danger of losing him. So we're delighted we managed to sign him."

– Sir Alex Ferguson

Name: Tiago Manuel Dias Correia (Bébé)
Position: Attacker
Born: 12/07/1990
Previous clubs: Estrela da Amadora, Vitoria de Guimaraes

Never before in his 24 years at Old Trafford has Sir Alex Ferguson signed a player without witnessing him in action, either live or on video, but the United manager bent the rules to enlist Portuguese attacker Bébé. The 20-year-old forward caught the eye of United's scouting network with his pre-season displays for Vitoria de Guimaraes in Portugal, and the Reds swooped to head off interest from a number of other clubs – snapping up Bébé before he could even play competitively for a club he had joined only five weeks earlier. "Sometimes you have to act on impulse," admitted Sir Alex. Fast, strong and versatile enough to play on either flank or centrally, Bébé brings a powerful unpredictability to the United attack, and follows the Reds' trend of recruiting talented youngsters and honing their unquestioned gifts.

He's two-footed, he's very quick, there's material there. He's raw material but I'm sure we can work with that. By getting younger players now – at 20 or 21 – they have time and we don't need to rush them. They can become the players we want them to be."

– Sir Alex Ferguson

Local Authority

The 2009/10 campaign heralded the evolution of the Manchester derby to the most anticipated fixture in the Premier League...

At a club with standards as high as United's, winning only one piece of silverware means 2009/10 will go down as a campaign tinged with disappointment.

Nevertheless, it was a season interspersed with unforgettable moments, and many of them came against local rivals Manchester City. As the season began, the sale of Cristiano Ronaldo and Carlos Tevez's cross-city switch at Eastlands prompted many giddy onlookers to suggest City would soon be overtaking United.

Inside the United camp, however, there was a determination to stay one step ahead of the Blues. "We know how much the derbies mean to the supporters, and they mean just as much to us," says Paul Scholes, who then did his level best to help put City firmly in their place. "Any victory against them is nice, and to beat them in injury time three times in one season was a very nice feeling."

"We had some unbelievable games against them," says Wayne Rooney. "Michael Owen's goal in the last minute at Old Trafford was a great moment,

and I really enjoyed scoring the winner against them in the Carling Cup semi-final to take us to Wembley. But Scholesy's winner was probably the best of the lot. You could hear their crowd go quiet and you could just hear our fans celebrating, that was the best. I was on the pitch, just running about!"

United's celebrations at Eastlands underlined the stoked feeling in a fixture which had been diluted by City's residence in United's shadow. The Reds have clocked up trophies at a similar rate to the Stretford End banner which counts the years since the Blues last clutched silverware. There were times, however, when the two clubs were more evenly matched and even jostled for honours.

In 1968, City pipped United to the First Division title, only for the Reds to trump that with victory in the European Cup final just over a fortnight later. Going into the 1970s, an increasingly ill-tempered fixture yielded several serious injuries, while City dominated results against a United team struggling to cope in the post-Sir Matt Busby era.

The balance of power swung back and forth throughout the 1980s, but United didn't lose a single derby in the 1990s and City sprung only occasional shocks after the turn of the millennium. In 2008, however, the arrival of the Abu Dhabi United Group inflated City's bank balance and ambition, and they now covet the finest players and biggest prizes.

"They've bought some fantastic players now, big name players and I think over the next few seasons they're going to be very difficult to play against," admits Wes Brown. "It happened with Chelsea and now it's happening with City, you can't ignore teams with that kind of investment. As a United fan, the competition's always good and I think there's even more of that to come."

"I don't want City to win anything," adds Rooney. "You don't want your closest rivals picking up trophies. The derbies have become more interesting and improved as spectacles now. I'm sure City will probably keep spending more money, but we just have to step our game up again and try to keep beating them!"

After United's 4-3 win over City in September 2009, Sir Alex Ferguson described the epic encounter as 'the best derby ever'. Given that each of the subsequent three games carried similar levels of drama, it seems safe to say that Manchester derbies will never be the same again.

The Road To Wembley

United successfully defended the Carling Cup in 2009/10 – here's how the Reds ensured further strain on the Old Trafford trophy cabinet…

A mundane affair was lit up by Danny Welbeck's excellent winner to seal United's spot in the fourth round. The striker swapped passes with Michael Owen before steering an unerring finish inside the far post on 66 minutes. Sir Alex Ferguson, who named senior squad debutants Joshua King and Magnus Eikrem on the bench, had earlier seen his side go down to ten men after Fabio was sent off for hauling down Michael Kightly as the last man just before the half-hour mark. Wolves' numerical advantage did little to galvanise their ambition in a game with few clear-cut chances. Thankfully, Welbeck made no mistake with his opportunity.

United: Kuszczak; Neville, Brown, J.Evans, Fabio; Nani, Gibson, Carrick, Welbeck (King 81); Owen (Valencia 69), Macheda (De Laet 31).

"It was great to play with Michael Owen. You can always learn from his movement, it's unbelievable. I just knew he was around the corner and he knew where I was going next. He played it there and I finished it off well." - Danny Welbeck

23.9.09 – Round 3
United 1 Wolves 0
(Welbeck)

The Reds' battling qualities were evident once again in overcoming the dismissal of skipper Gary Neville to earn a 2-0 win at Oakwell. United, who started with debutant Gabriel Obertan, got off to the perfect start when Danny Welbeck buried a free header from Anderson's corner on six minutes. The Tykes weren't about to roll over though and Daniel Bogdanovic was unlucky to see his header thump against Ben Foster's post. Any hopes the home side had of a comeback were dashed just before the hour thanks to a masterclass in finishing from Michael Owen, who bypassed three defenders before calmly curling the ball home.

United: Foster; Neville, Brown, J.Evans, Fabio; Obertan, Anderson, Rafael, Welbeck (Tosic 53); Owen (De Laet 65), Macheda.

"We didn't play as well as we could have, especially in the first half when we were average. But we're happy to be through and I was pleased to score." - Michael Owen

27.10.09 – Round 4
Barnsley 0 United 2
(Welbeck, Owen)

32

01.12.09 – Quarter-final
United 2 Tottenham 0
(Gibson 2)

A youthful Reds side progressed to the last four of the competition thanks to two excellent strikes from the ever-improving Darron Gibson. Having been criticised a few days earlier for a disappointing Champions League display against Besiktas, Sir Alex's youngsters proved their class against a strong Spurs team with Gibson in particular catching the eye, and not just for his superb double. The Irish international showed good awareness and determination in United's engine room, and capped a fine display with a couple of accomplished finishes from outside the area.

United: Kuszczak; Neville, Brown, Vidic, De Laet; Park, Anderson (Tosic 82), Gibson, Obertan (Carrick 62); Welbeck, Berbatov (Macheda 62).

"Spurs have established Premier League players and I think there was pressure on the young lads to prove we are good enough to play at their level. We showed we're capable of doing that." - Darron Gibson

19.01.10 – Semi-final 1
Manchester City 2 United 1 (Giggs)

Sir Alex fielded a tellingly strong side as the Carling Cup holders came up against a City side determined to reach Wembley and claim a trophy for the first time in 34 years. United's early dominance was rewarded with a 17th minute goal from Ryan Giggs, but fellow Welshman Craig Bellamy helped draw the home side level after winning a controversial penalty at the expense of Rafael. Former United striker Carlos Tevez rammed home the spot-kick, and then struck again on 65 minutes to head home from close range and stoke City's dreams of silverware.

United: Van der Sar; Rafael (Diouf 90), Brown, J.Evans, Evra; Valencia (Scholes 88), Fletcher, Carrick, Anderson (Owen 72), Giggs; Rooney.

"We got off to the perfect start, but after we scored we probably weren't as crisp with our passing and kept playing the ball backwards. We let City back into it, really." - Ryan Giggs

27.01.10 – Semi-final 2 – United 3 Manchester City 1
(Scholes, Carrick, Rooney) United win 4-3 on aggregate

Yet another incredible Manchester derby was decided by an injury-time winner in front of the Stretford End, as the Reds booked a trip to the Carling Cup final for the second season running. Paul Scholes and Michael Carrick got Old Trafford rocking when they put United ahead in the tie after the break, but Tevez's flicked finish soon after drew City level on aggregate. The tie looked to be heading for extra-time until Giggs' inviting cross was powered home by the head of Wayne Rooney in the dying seconds, prompting frenzied scenes of celebration. The Reds had another shot at a pot, while the Blues went home empty-handed.

"When Tevez scored, it took the steam out of us for ten minutes and we were all expecting extra time, but then Giggsy put in another great delivery and Wazza popped up with an unbelievable winner." - Darren Fletcher

United: Van der Sar; Rafael (Brown 74), J.Evans, Ferdinand, Evra; Fletcher, Carrick, Scholes, Giggs, Nani (Valencia 90); Rooney.

Carling Cup Final

28 February 2010, Wembley Stadium, Attendance: 88,596

MANCHESTER UNITED 2
Owen 12, Rooney 74

ASTON VILLA 1
Milner 5 (pen)

Sir Alex reflects on a historic day as the Reds come from behind to retain a cup for the first time in the club's history…

"It was a great achievement by the players and winning a trophy is always a fantastic feeling. We were made to work very hard for it though and Villa deserve a lot of credit for the way they performed.

"The first half was a real ding-dong battle, it was a soft tiring pitch and it took its toll on the players. I was hoping we could get some tempo into our game because in the first ten minutes Villa laid down the gauntlet to us and made us turn towards our own goal.

"I don't think there was any doubt about their penalty when Nemanja [Vidic] brought Gabriel Agbonlahor down after five minutes. As for whether he should have been dismissed or not, I think we got a lucky break there, he was the last man and could easily have been sent off.

"If you go a goal down early in a cup final you've got a job to do and you need a lot of patience. Thankfully we kept our cool and once we scored we looked a lot stronger.

"Michael [Owen] got us back into it with a fine finish. He deserved his goal - I thought he was one of our best performers in the first half. Unfortunately, he had to go off just before half-time with an injury that was to rule him out for the rest of the season. He hadn't had a lot of football up to that point and the Wembley pitch probably wasn't the best for him. Unfortunately, he paid the penalty for it.

"Thankfully we had a pretty good replacement in Wayne Rooney and he went on to score the winner with another excellent header. The technique he showed to loop the ball over the top of Friedel was fantastic.

"It was a great day out for everyone connected to the club, particularly the fans whose support was superb as always. Whenever we really need them, they are there and we were delighted to reward them with a trophy."

34

The Teams

MANCHESTER UNITED

Kuszczak; Rafael (Neville 66), Vidic, Evans, Evra; Valencia, Carrick, Fletcher, Park (Gibson 85); Berbatov, Owen (Rooney 42).

Subs not used: Foster, Brown, Scholes, Diouf

Booked: Vidic, Evra

ASTON VILLA

Friedel; Cuellar (Carew 80), Collins, Dunne, Warnock; A Young, Milner, Petrov, Downing; Agbonlahor, Heskey.
Subs not used: Guzan, L Young, Beye, Sidwell, Delph, Delfouneso
Booked: Collins, Downing

"It's not nice to get injured and know you will be out for weeks, rather than days. But you can't disguise the pleasure you get from scoring, winning a match and picking up a trophy. You remember days like that for the rest of your life."

Michael Owen

"The Carling Cup has been a really good competition to us in the last few years and it's always great to get a medal around your neck early on in the season."

Gary Neville

"After going behind early on we had to get the ball down and keep believing in ourselves. Villa are a great team on the counterattack but we showed great courage to come back and win the game."

Darren Fletcher

"We always believed we could go on to win. We just had to be patient and trust each other. It was a first Carling Cup victory for me and a dream to win at Wembley."

Michael Carrick

"I knew a few days before I wouldn't be starting because of a sore knee and stomach bug, but I felt better on the day and was champing at the bit to get on. It was a great feeling to play in a final at Wembley and to score the winning goal was unbelievable."

Wayne Rooney

35

Wazza's 10 of the Best

During the course of 2009/10, Wayne Rooney established himself as one of the world's greatest players, scoring 34 goals - his best tally for a campaign - and leading the line with distinction. Here, we pick his top 10 goals of the season...

United 5 Wigan 0

Barclays Premier League, 30 December 2009

Wigan must be sick of the sight of Rooney. By the end of 2009/10 the striker had nine goals in eleven games against the Latics, and his ninth was a pearler. Latching onto Rafael's superb right-wing cross, Rooney's powerful swept volley gave goalkeeper Chris Kirkland no chance.

United 2 Blackburn 0

Barclays Premier League, 31 October 2009

Part of Rooney's evolution into an all-round goal menace has been his ability to shoot with his weaker foot. Here, he ran onto Anderson's low cross and whipped a superb left-footed half-volley across Paul Robinson and into the far corner to secure victory.

United 3 Manchester City 1

Carling Cup semi-final, second leg 27 January 2010

One of Rooney's simplest finishes of the season, but the magnitude of the goal earns it a place on this list. In added time (again), breaking City's hearts when they were within touching distance of a first trophy in 34 years, it's little surprise Rooney's close-range header sparked such wild celebrations.

United 3 Fulham 0

Barclays Premier League, 14 March 2010

The perfect team goal. Every outfield player touched the ball during a spell of fine possession football. It really clicked into overdrive when Dimitar Berbatov showed a Velcro touch to bring down Michael Carrick's long pass, motored past two defenders and pulled back for Rooney to sweep home his finish.

United 4 AC Milan 0

Champions League last 16, second leg, 10 March 2010

Wayne just wouldn't leave Milan alone, plundering four goals in two games against the Rossoneri. This was the one which made victory certain, coming just after half-time at Old Trafford. Nani's measured pass around the back of the Milan defence fell perfectly for Rooney to impishly stab home at the Stretford End.

United 3 West Ham 0

Barclays Premier League, 23 February 2010
A sublime team goal which carried a devastating simplicity. Dimitar Berbatov was meandering along in possession and then, three touches later, the ball was in the net. A fine ball from the Bulgarian to Antonio Valencia, a perfect first-time volleyed cross by the Ecuadorian and a thumping header from Rooney to finish.

Tottenham 1 United 3

Barclays Premier League, 12 September 2009
With United a goal ahead but a man down after Paul Scholes' dismissal, Rooney made the game safe with a superb solo goal. Latching onto Darren Fletcher's searching pass, Rooney picked up the ball, cut inside, nutmegged Alan Hutton and slipped a low shot in-between Carlo Cudicini's legs. Stunning.

AC Milan 2 United 3

Champions League last 16, first leg, 16 February 2010
The Reds had never won at the San Siro or even managed a goal there against AC Milan. Paul Scholes altered the latter with his equaliser, before Rooney set up United's maiden victory in the stadium with two fine headers. His first, back-pedalling, then rising to loop a finish into the far top corner was a masterpiece.

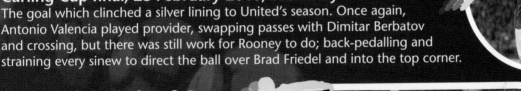

Aston Villa 1 United 2

Carling Cup final, 28 February 2010, Wembley
The goal which clinched a silver lining to United's season. Once again, Antonio Valencia played provider, swapping passes with Dimitar Berbatov and crossing, but there was still work for Rooney to do; back-pedalling and straining every sinew to direct the ball over Brad Friedel and into the top corner.

Arsenal 1 United 3

Barclays Premier League, 31 January 2010
United's impressive victory at the Emirates in January was largely built on rapid counter-attacks, and this particularly devastating instance won the club's Goal of the Season award. Rooney controlled Park's chip, fed Nani and then sprinted over 70 yards to take the return pass and smash it past Manuel Almunia.

Rooney's favourite goal of the season came at the Emirates
"I think it was the best I scored. Most of my goals last season were tap-ins or headers so it was nice to be a bit more involved in the build-up for a goal like that. It was a quick break and I was a bit tired at the end of the run! It's always nice to score against Arsenal and the goal came at an important time in the game, to make it 2-0. I was delighted with it."

Gunners goal is Wayne's pick

United Oscars

Player Awards

And the winner is... we go behind-the-scenes at the club awards night

Since 2006, United's annual Player of the Year awards have been a highlight in the season's calendar – and 2010 was no exception. The entire coaching and playing staff were once again given the red carpet treatment at the glitzy gala event, but it was Wayne Rooney who unsurprisingly stole the show.

The ceremony, which takes place in Old Trafford's Manchester Suite and is broadcast live on MUTV, caters for over 800 guests and raises vital funds for the Manchester United Foundation. Moreover, it is a celebration of a season's work and recognition for those who have excelled.

As expected, Rooney swept the 2010 board, picking up the Sir Matt Busby Player of the Year award, the Players' Player of the Year accolade and the Goal of the Season prize for his breathtaking breakaway strike at Arsenal's Emirates Stadium.

"It's fantastic to get the votes from your team-mates. Last season was definitely my best at United - I played well and became more consistent in my goalscoring, which is something I wanted to do."

"It's a special feeling to get an award from the fans and something I'm really proud of. They come and watch us all over the country and Europe and the support they give us is unbelievable. They're the best fans in the world."

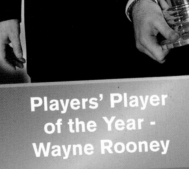

Players' Player of the Year - Wayne Rooney

"I was a bit surprised to win this - I thought Michael Owen's winner against Manchester City should have got it! The Arsenal goal was the best I scored last season - most of my goals were tap-ins or headers so it was nice to be a bit more involved in the build-up for a goal like that."

Sir Matt Busby Player of the Year - Wayne Rooney

Goal of the Season - Wayne Rooney

United's top scorer for the 2009/10 campaign won the Sir Matt Busby award, as voted for by Reds fans all over the world, by a landslide after receiving 83% of the votes cast on ManUtd.com – his second such honour following his original success in 2006. Patrice Evra and Antonio Valencia were in second and third place respectively.

Rooney wasn't the only winner on the night – Ritchie De Laet scooped the Denzil Haroun Reserve Player of the Year title, while William Keane collected the Jimmy Murphy Young Player of the Year award. It was a silver-laden 24 hours for the pair, who had helped the Reserves overcome Aston Villa in the Reserve League Play-Off final at Old Trafford the previous day.

"Ritchie has been a revelation since signing from Stoke and he deservedly gained some first team appearances last season. He is a very versatile defender who also has an eye for a goal, and he's a real leader in the team."

Ole Gunnar Solskjaer – Reserves manager

Denzil Haroun Reserve Team Player of the Year – Ritchie De Laet

De Laet saw off competition from the coaching staff's other nominees, Magnus Eikrem and Oliver Gill, while Keane finished above fellow nominees Nicky Ajose and Scott Wootton in the fans' poll.

"Will has been such a smooth operator in his first year. He's been really outstanding and scored some stunning goals but his general team play and his demeanour, his attitude on and off the pitch, have been excellent."

Paul McGuinness – U18s manager

Jimmy Murphy Young Player of the Year – Will Keane

Live in your
living room

MUTV's Mandy Henry has presented the last five Player of the Year ceremonies since the inaugural event in 2006. She gives us the lowdown on what goes on behind the cameras...

What do you most enjoy about presenting the awards?

It's one of my favourite parts of the whole season as far as presenting at MUTV goes. It's a chance for everyone to get dressed up and celebrate the success that individual players have had at all levels at the club.

How much preparation goes into planning the event?

From a technical point of view it takes months of planning, as it's one of the biggest events that we cover on the channel. I get involved a few weeks before, when I prepare some statistics on the nominees and have a think about what to ask potential winners.

How long are you actually on air for?

This time, it was from 7.30pm until just after 11pm. It may not sound that long, but in terms of presenting totally unscripted and adlibbing for three and a half hours, it's a very long time! Nevertheless, I absolutely love doing it and the adrenalin helps keep you going.

Has anything ever gone wrong?

The first year I presented the awards we had planned to show footage of the players arriving right at the start, and I was supposed to talk over the shots. Unfortunately, there was a technical glitch so I couldn't see the pictures on the monitor in the studio that I was supposed to follow and didn't have a clue who viewers at home were seeing!

You have the great job of interviewing the winners and a number of special guests on the MUTV couch...

For me, that's the crucial element in the evening being a success. Viewers at home want to see and hear from the players, whether it's an up-and-coming youngster who has excelled at academy level or Wayne Rooney who won everything last season.

And Sir Alex always pops in for a quick chat too...

Yes, the boss and I have a fantastic working relationship and every year he's always very relaxed on the sofa. He gives us the odd story now and again - during last season's awards he revealed that Jonny Evans had signed a new contract which was a great exclusive for MUTV.

Strength in Reserve

The Reds' burgeoning youngsters heaped more strain on the club's trophy cabinet during the 2009/10 campaign...

United's first team may have fallen agonisingly short of a fourth consecutive league title, but there was still cause for celebration at Carrington as the Reds' Reserves and Academy sides topped their respective divisions.

Ole Gunnar Solskjaer and Warren Joyce's second string brought the title back to Old Trafford for the first time in four seasons with an extremely impressive campaign, and then went on to edge a thrilling national playoff against southern division champions Aston Villa.

In typical United fashion, the Reserves attained glory in the most dramatic of circumstances, trailing three times in a six-goal thriller, before snaring the national playoff shield after a nerve-shredding penalty shootout.

"It's always dramatic, with United," says Solskjaer. "The attitude of the boys against Villa, and all season long, was brilliant. That's part of being a United player. You need talent and skill and all that, but character and attitude are things Sir Alex is always looking for in players.

"The very best have got great talent, but they've also got that character. The big game mentality, the winning mentality. They're humble. They always want to improve, they're never satisfied, they're hungry to be even better. The ones who get complacent, who are happy because they've won a trophy, they haven't got the character for United. You need the strength of character to bounce back from setbacks and never give in. That's the history of this club and I think these boys have shown they can be a part of it."

As if the future wasn't bright enough, Paul McGuinness' under-18 stars also caught the eye in winning the Academy League regional division. The Reds finished comfortably clear of second-placed Everton to book a place in the national finals, where four regional winners went through to knockout encounters. Although Arsenal edged a thrilling draw and subsequent penalty shootout at Carrington to reach the final and retain the national crown, there was still plenty of cause for cheer.

Having shone at under-18 level, a host of the Reds' youngsters will step up into Solskjaer's Reserves in the near future, and the Norwegian relishes the chance to help such talented players further themselves.

"I think that's one of the exciting things about this job: you have so many good players," says Ole. "You want to be able to work with talented players and test their characters. You see their quality every day in training, but I don't see every game and it's interesting to get to know how they handle different scenarios. We've got a great bunch of lads coming through now and I'm really looking forward to working with them."

Twinkling talents

Here are five youngsters who are on their way through the Reds' ranks...

Name: Tom Cleverley

Born: 12 August 1989; Basingstoke

Position: Midfielder

The oldest member of the quintet, but one bursting to step into the first team fold. In his limited experience of three pre-seasons with the senior squad, Cleverley caught the eye and found the net in both campaigns. Now, having flourished in a season-long loan at Watford, Tom is recognised as one of England's brightest young talents. Internationally recognised at under-21 level, the intelligent, goal-getting midfielder is facing a crucial campaign as he aims to crack the big time.

Name: Will Keane

Born: 11 January 1993; Stockport

Position: Striker

Named Jimmy Murphy Young Player of the Year for 2009/10, it's fair to say Will Keane was one of the outstanding stories of last term for the Reds. Having enjoyed a goal-laden season for the under-18s, Keane made a seamless step up to Reserve team duty. Working under another arch-poacher, Ole Gunnar Solskjaer, Will's undoubted talent flourished. He is a natural finisher, has tremendous speed of thought and understanding of the game, and has already been tipped for big things by Sir Alex.

Strength in Reserve

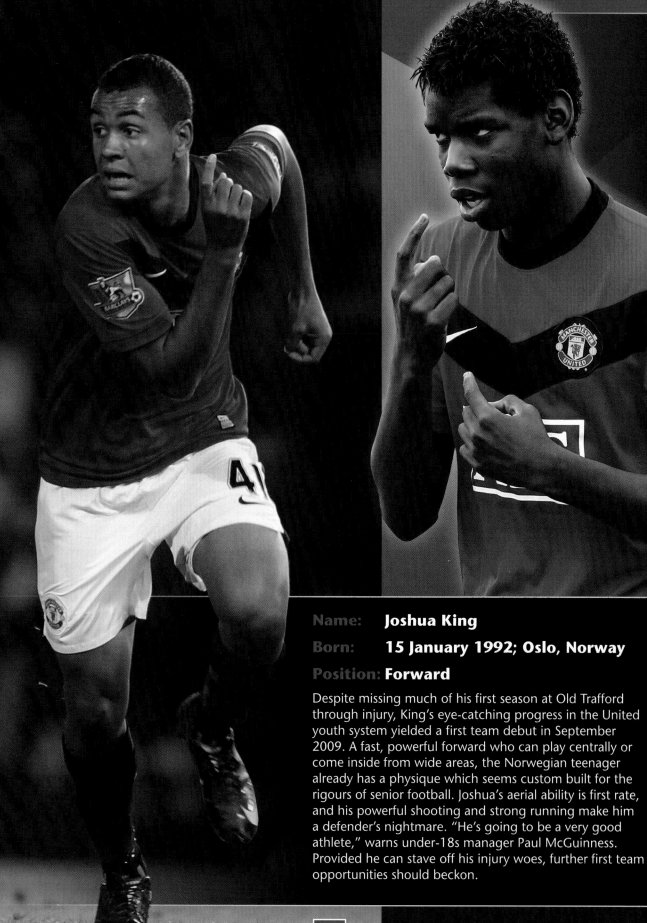

Name: **Joshua King**

Born: **15 January 1992; Oslo, Norway**

Position: **Forward**

Despite missing much of his first season at Old Trafford through injury, King's eye-catching progress in the United youth system yielded a first team debut in September 2009. A fast, powerful forward who can play centrally or come inside from wide areas, the Norwegian teenager already has a physique which seems custom built for the rigours of senior football. Joshua's aerial ability is first rate, and his powerful shooting and strong running make him a defender's nightmare. "He's going to be a very good athlete," warns under-18s manager Paul McGuinness. Provided he can stave off his injury woes, further first team opportunities should beckon.

Twinkling talents

Name: Paul Pogba

Born: 15 March 1993;
Lagny Sur Marne,
France

Position: Midfielder

Having arrived at Old Trafford amid a furious reaction from his previous club, Le Havre, Paul knew his performances in England would be heavily scrutinised. Fortunately, it soon became clear that he has the temperament to cope.
The towering French youngster will undoubtedly fill out physically, further equipping him for life in midfield, but his natural talent shines like a beacon. His tackling, passing and shooting are all carried off with a supreme elegance, and his speed of thought and vision mark him out from his peers.

Name: Ryan Tunnicliffe

Born: 30 December 1992; Bury

Position: Defender / Midfielder

A squat, stocky presence, it would be easy to dismiss Ryan as a tough-tackler on first impressions. However, while he admittedly relishes the chance to contest a challenge with any opponent, he is also blessed with terrific ability, energy and ball-playing skills. A midfielder by trade, Tunnicliffe can also operate with great competence and intelligence across the backline. After two impressive seasons with McGuinness' under-18s, expect Ryan to have an impact on Solskjaer's Reserves during the 2010/11 campaign.

Enduring Excellence

It's extremely rare for a player to carve out a career spanning over 15 years at Old Trafford, but United's current squad boasts three of them. With over 2,000 United appearances between them, Ryan Giggs, Gary Neville and Paul Scholes are living club legends.

Three of the Reds' all-time top five appearance-makers, Giggs, Neville and Scholes made their senior debuts in 1991, 1992 and 1994 respectively, and have been almost permanent fixtures in Sir Alex Ferguson's first team ever since. Along the way, they have picked up 74 winners' medals in all senior competitions.

Even in their mid-30s, the trio remain a key part of Sir Alex's plans, and penned one-year contract extensions during the 2009/10 season. According to Eric Harrison, the coach credited with nurturing them through United's youth system, their sustained success comes from the effort which prompted their promotion all those years ago.

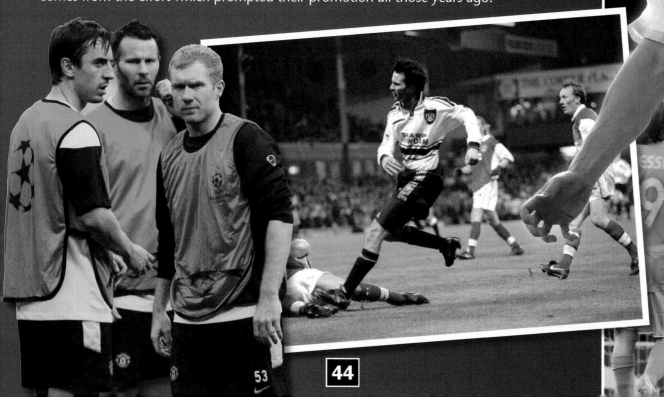

"Talent is one thing but determination and dedication are the two extra watchwords that make the big difference," says Harrison. "Unless you have dedication and determination then you will never have a career like those three guys.

"If any of them had been lacking in one of those departments then they wouldn't be still up where they are now. They were a very easy group to coach. Their whole object in life was to play in Manchester United's first team and it drove them on.

"If ever you thought you'd made it then you would be history at United. They didn't come in every day scared to death, but they knew the demands and responded. That environment built into them this attitude that has kept them going well into their 30s."

HONOURS LIST

Ryan Giggs (31 trophies)

1 FIFA Club World Cup
1 Intercontinental Cup
2 UEFA Champions League titles
1 UEFA Super Cup
11 Premier League titles
4 FA Cups
3 League Cups
8 Community Shields

Paul Scholes (23 trophies)

1 FIFA Club World Cup
1 Intercontinental Cup
2 UEFA Champions League titles
9 Premier League titles
3 FA Cups
2 League Cups
5 Community Shields

Gary Neville (20 trophies)

1 FIFA Club World Cup
1 Intercontinental Cup
2 UEFA Champions League titles
8 Premier League titles
3 FA Cups
2 League Cups
3 Community Shields

Enduring Excellence

In Sir Alex, the trio have worked under a father figure who has overseen their evolution from promising young talents to silver-dripped veterans, and their appreciation of him is limitless.

"The boss is the reason we're still at the club, and the reason we were given an opportunity in the first place," insists Neville. "He promoted youth all those years ago, sorted out the youth set-up and has pushed it ever since. We're soldiers, if you like, and we're happy to do a job for him that makes him want to keep us.

"There's still an opportunity for us here and we want to carry on winning season upon season. Playing for this club is the best thing in the world and we've been doing it for a long time now. We still feel as though there are contributions to be made on and off the pitch, and so does the manager – which is the most important thing."

A glance back at the 2009/10 season validates the importance of Giggs, Neville and Scholes, as they clocked up 98 appearances between them and were especially prominent towards the end of the season, as the manager sought to utilise their vast experience.

The three, who are close friends, have been in the winning habit for well over a decade, so it's far from surprising that Sir Alex is keen to retain them all as members of his coaching staff when they do finally decide to retire. "They are the living proof for young players that the United system allows players to succeed," says the boss. "When they stop playing, they will stay. All three are taking their coaching diplomas and I don't think the club will pass up that much experience."

In the meantime, however, Sir Alex will be hoping their know-how can bring yet more silverware during the 2010/11 campaign.

Scholes on Giggs

"Giggsy's amazing. His goalscoring, his appearances and the way he's played in the vast majority of those games. He's been probably the best player this club's ever had. Hopefully he'll be recognised in that way when he calls it a day."

Giggs on Neville

"Nev does his research on the players he's up against and he's fantastic at doing a job on his opponent. He's a great professional and a top defender, and he also gives you a lot going forward as an attacking player as well."

Neville on Scholes

"Scholesy is still a brilliant player. He controls the pace of a game for us, everything sticks with him and he never wastes a pass. He's a fantastic, world class player and he's crucially important to the squad."

When it comes to getting ready for the start of the new campaign the pre-season tour is really important. It can be hard work, but going over to America was brilliant. The weather was good and we visited some great cities. It's not as hectic as some places we travel to and things are a little bit more relaxed because not everybody recognises us so we're able to go for a wander and do a bit of shopping!

We flew to Chicago for the first part of our trip and had a good week of training. We trained in front of our fans in one session at MLS side Chicago Fire's stadium and we were given a great reception. Soccer is getting bigger all the time in the States and so many kids are playing the game now. I can only see it getting more popular which is great.

As well as training, we also took time out to meet supporters at various events, which is always enjoyable. One such visit marked the launch of our new home kit which me, Berba, Sheasy, Gabby Obertan and Giggsy went along to. We all really like the new strip and hopefully we'll have a lot of success in it over the coming months.

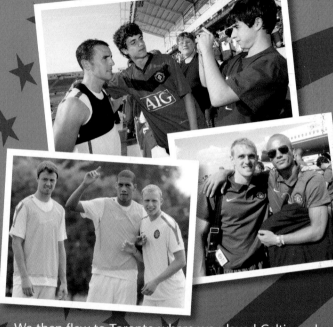

We then flew to Toronto where we played Celtic and it was definitely good to get a game under our belts and get back into the swing of things. It was a good result for us – we won 3-1 – and I was pleased to get some minutes on the clock. I came on at half-time and played alongside one of our new signings Chris Smalling. Chris is a great lad and he fitted in brilliantly from the start. The tours are a chance for the young lads to show the manager what they can do and it was good to see Danny Welbeck and Tom Cleverley do just that and get on the score-sheet against Celtic.

We were really pleased to kick off our pre-season preparations with a win and it rounded off a great first week of the tour.

The victory over Celtic in Toronto was an enjoyable game to be involved in and it was great to be back playing again after a long summer. On a personal level, captaining the team was a great honour. It's a privilege to pull on the red shirt any time, but being a Scottish lad, to skipper the lads against Celtic meant I was even more desperate to win the match.

The following day we headed to Philadelphia, which was our base for the second week of the trip. The training throughout the tour was very intense with double sessions most days in very humid conditions, but it provided us with great preparation for the new season. The facilities at the Novacare training complex, which is home to American football team Philadelphia Eagles, were absolutely first class.

A trip to Philly wouldn't be complete without a visit to the 'Rocky Steps.' The 72 steps, which lie in front of the entrance to the Philadelphia Museum of Art, became famous after their appearance in the triple-Oscar-winning film starring Sylvester Stallone. Growing up it was one of the films I watched over and over, and being a sportsman you can relate to the character so it was a great experience to visit such a famous landmark. Me and Wes had been talking about running up the steps beforehand but he chickened out! Still, Nani and Edwin did their best Rocky impressions at the top.

We were pleased to secure a second tour victory over Philadelphia Union. They made things difficult for us at times, but Gabby Obertan scored a good goal to win us the game 1-0. The following day myself, Ryan, Paul, Edwin and the manager travelled to New York to attend Hublot's 'Million Dollar Challenge' event on 5th Avenue which raised over $100,000 for UNICEF.

The week in Philadelphia was extremely enjoyable and most importantly we made good progress with our fitness, which is the whole purpose of pre-season.

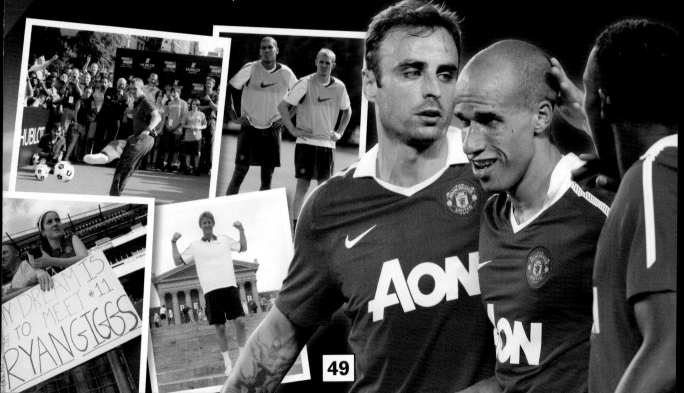

Reds on Tour

All the lads had been particularly looking forward to going to Kansas City and then onto Houston because, for many of us in the squad, it was the first time we'd been to either place.

The support we had in Kansas City was fantastic. Despite a bad thunderstorm on the day we arrived, the fans came out in their hundreds to watch us train. Before the session started I met up with Kansas City Wizards striker Kei Kamara, who is from Sierra Leone. We chatted about my visit to the country with UNICEF at the end of 2009 and also talked about the game at the Arrowsmith Stadium the following day.

The match was our third of the tour, so we expected our fitness to be at a good level and hoped we'd be close to reaching our best in terms of performance. Unfortunately, things didn't turn out that way with the Wizards beating us 2-1. It's always disappointing when you lose, no matter whether it's a friendly or a competitive game. While the Wizards deserved credit for their performance, quite simply we didn't play well. Their second goal just before half-time was a killer, especially as it came so quickly after we'd got ourselves back into it.

Quite a few of the young lads started the match and although it wasn't a great day for us, the experience of playing at a fantastic stadium, in front of a good crowd against good opposition will have helped them. You learn something from every game you play when you're younger and you always try to take something from it even when you lose. They will definitely be better for the experience.

Houston
– Edwin van der Sar

Our new team-mate Javier 'Chicharito' Hernandez was waiting for us when we got to Houston. It was nice to meet him and he came with a few of us to the Texas Children's Hospital after our first training session. One of the best parts of our job is being able to go out and meet our fans - young and old - and being able to bring a smile to the faces of those who are having a difficult time means a lot.

One of the highlights of the whole tour was our visit to NASA's Johnson Space Center. We were shown around the Mission Control Center, before being taken to a space hangar where a full-size replica of a shuttle is housed. I'm not sure how it happened but the three goalkeepers were chosen to try on some of the astronaut gear! Overall, it was a great experience.

We were told before we came to Houston that a Premier League team had never won the All-Star game across 90 minutes, so that was a real incentive for us. We also wanted to respond well after the defeat in Kansas City.

We changed the system a little bit against the All-Stars and went with a 4-3-3 and I think it worked well. We scored some top quality goals in the 5-2 victory and we were all delighted to see Chicharito get himself on the score-sheet in his first game for the club. Even in training he looked very sharp, with a good eye for goal. You could see his quality from the first chance he had just before he scored, while the finish for his goal was tremendous.

All in all it was a great night for us. To play an All-Star game in front of a great crowd and get the win was a good experience and a fantastic way to end the tour.

Soccer Aid

A number of familiar faces trod the Old Trafford turf in the name of charity in 2010

Visitors to Old Trafford are used to seeing Sir Alex's men strutting their stuff on matchday, but those in attendance at Soccer Aid and United Relief Live saw some of the game's greatest-ever players line up alongside a host of celebrity football fans to raise money for the Manchester United Foundation and its charity partners. Every superstar was desperate to win, but more importantly fun and fundraising took centre stage…

It's not every day you see Ryan Giggs on the same side as Austin Powers or witness Robbie Williams tackling Zinedine Zidane, but Old Trafford played host to both scenarios during the Soccer Aid match between England and the Rest of the World in June.

Famous faces from the sport and entertainment worlds came together in a bid to raise money for global children's charity UNICEF – who work closely with the Foundation – and entertain a 65,000-strong crowd at the Theatre of Dreams.

Hollywood actor Woody Harrelson ensured a first Soccer Aid victory for the ROW after slotting home the winning spot-kick during an enthralling penalty shoot-out.

Earlier, the ROW, featuring the predictably outstanding Giggs and Zidane, had come from two goals down to secure a 2-2 draw. Jamie Redknapp put dad Harry's England side ahead on the stroke of half-

time after some lovely link-up play with former Red Teddy Sheringham and Alan Shearer.

Sheringham doubled the advantage on the hour-mark with a firm header in front of the Stretford End, but the ROW pulled one back through Joe Calzaghe soon after. Former Liverpool defender Sami Hyypia netted an equaliser 12 minutes from time when he rose to meet a Luis Figo corner.

Despite an inspired display during the shoot-out from Man of the Match and England stopper Jamie Theakston, who saved four spot-kicks, Harrelson claimed the trophy for Kenny Dalglish's side for the first time in three attempts as the ROW ran out 7-6 winners.

> "Captaining the Rest of The World to victory was unbelievable – you can forget the Oscars, this is the trophy I wanted to get my hands on."
>
> *Michael Sheen, actor*

ENGLAND 2
Redknapp 45, Sheringham 60

REST OF THE WORLD 2
Calzaghe 64, Hyypia 78

ROW win 7-6 on penalties

ENGLAND

Harry Redknapp (Manager),
James Corden (Assistant Manager),
Bryan Robson (Coach)

Celebrities

Captain - Robbie Williams (singer)
Dominic Cooper (actor)
Ricky Hatton (boxer)
Damian Lewis (actor)
Ralf Little (actor)
Paddy McGuinness (comedian)
Olly Murs (singer)
Rupert Penry-Jones (actor)
Ben Shephard (TV presenter)
Jamie Theakston (TV presenter)
Bradley Walsh (actor)
Jonathan Wilkes (actor)

Legends

Nicky Butt	Teddy Sheringham
Martin Keown	Alan Shearer
Jamie Redknapp	David Seaman

REST OF THE WORLD

Kenny Dalglish (Manager),
Ian Rush (Assistant Manager),
Eric Harrison (Coach)

Celebrities

Captain - Michael Sheen (actor)
Simon Baker (actor)
Nicky Byrne (singer)
Joe Calzaghe (boxer)
Shane Filan (singer)
Woody Harrelson (actor)
Gethin Jones (TV presenter)
Patrick Kielty (comedian)
James Kyson-Lee (actor)
Brian Lara (ex-cricketer)
Mike Myers (actor)
Gordon Ramsay (TV chef)

Legends

Luis Figo	Henrik Larsson
Ryan Giggs	Jens Lehmann
Sami Hyypia	Zinedine Zidane

"As a huge United fan stepping out on the hallowed turf at Old Trafford was amazing and to play alongside Giggsy – a United legend – was unbelievable. The memories will stay with me forever."

- Nicky Byrne, Westlife

United Relief Live

The inaugural United Relief Live event provided an entertainment cocktail of football and music at Old Trafford, raising vital funds for the Foundation and Sport Relief and reuniting a number of the club's 1999 Treble winners.

Jaap Stam, Ole Gunnar Solskjaer, Andrew Cole, Dwight Yorke, Ronny Johnsen and Denis Irwin were back in unison again alongside a host of celebrity Reds including Boyzone's Ronan Keating, 2009 X Factor runner-up Olly Murs and actor Max Beesley. The United XI took on a side made up of ex-opposition players and supporters, including former Liverpool pair Ian Rush and Peter Beardsley and comedian and City fan Jason Manford.

The day was kicked-off by United fan Tinchy Stryder, who was also part of the Reds' side, with The Hoosiers, The Saturdays and legendary crooner Tony Christie also

MANCHESTER UNITED XI 2
Ehiogu 55 (og), Fortune 90 (pen)

THE RIVALS 2
Little 46, Ehiogu 52

The Rivals win 5-4 on penalties

UNITED RELIEF live
The Big Red Day Out.

WINNERS

UNITED RELIEF live
The Big Red Day Out.

MANCHESTER UNITED XI

Legends

Clayton Blackmore
Andrew Cole
Quinton Fortune
Denis Irwin (Captain)
Ronny Johnsen
Lee Martin
Brian McClair
Pascal Olmeta
Andy Ritchie
Jaap Stam
Lee Sharpe
Ole Gunnar Solskjaer
Gary Walsh
Dwight Yorke

Celebrities

Max Beesley (actor)
Angus Deayton (TV presenter)
Keith Duffy (singer)
Ronan Keating (singer)
Olly Murs (singer)
Tinchy Stryder (rapper)
Ricky Whittle (actor)

THE RIVALS

Legends

Dave Beasant
Peter Beardsley
Dean Holdsworth
Ian Rush (Captain)
Alan Thompson
Ugo Ehiogu
Des Walker

Celebrities

Austin Healey (ex-rugby player)
George Lamb (Radio and TV presenter)
Ralf Little (actor)
Tim Lovejoy (TV presenter)
Lee Mack (comedian)
Jason Manford (comedian)
Paddy McGuinness (comedian)

> "Whenever footballers get together that competitive edge always comes out and you saw that at United Relief. We all wanted to win, but unfortunately the luck was with The Rivals in the shoot-out!"
>
> *Denis Irwin, United XI captain*

> "It was great to be back - I loved my time at United and I felt the same buzz when I put the shirt on again. It's a shame we didn't win, but just being back was a fantastic feeling."
>
> *Jaap Stam, former defender*

performing during the pre-match concert. Sir Alex Ferguson greeted both teams before kick-off, while, at half-time, Sir Bobby Charlton donned the red shirt once more to score a penalty in front of East Stand and Britain's Got Talent dance troupe Flawless entertained the crowd.

After a goalless first half, the Rivals made the breakthrough just after the restart through United fan Ralf Little. Having doubled the lead for his side soon after, former Aston Villa defender Ugo Ehiogu then found the net at the wrong end to give United a lifeline. The Reds drew level through an injury-time penalty from Quinton Fortune meaning, like Soccer Aid, the match would be decided on penalties.

Despite a brilliant performance from United goalkeeper Pascal Olmeta, who saved four spot-kicks, the Rivals came out on top after ex-Chelsea stopper Dave Beasant denied actor Ricky Whittle in sudden-death to seal a 5-4 win.

Spot the Difference

Can you spot the 7 differences between the two photographs?

Answers on page 62

Spot The (real) Ball

Can you guess which is the real ball in this photograph as Neville and Fletcher try to win possession at Goodison Park? Check your answer with the one on page 62.

Answer on page 62

True or False

1. Rio Ferdinand runs his own record label

True ☐ False ☐

4. Edwin van der Sar won the Champions League with Ajax before he won it with United.

True ☐ False ☐

2. Wayne Rooney scored his first United goal against his former club Everton.

True ☐ False ☐

5. Patrice Evra is one of 25 brothers and sisters.

True ☐ False ☐

3. Ryan Giggs attended Manchester City's School of Excellence as a teenager.

True ☐ False ☐

6. John O'Shea and Darren Fletcher share the same birthday.

True ☐ False ☐

Answers on page 62

ANAGRAMS

Unscramble the anagrams below to reveal the names of 10 United players...

1 Annoy Eye Row

2 Central Herd Ref

3 Saggy Grin

4 Far Salad Alive

5 So Van Jenny

6 Invaders Wander

7 Broad Snoring

8 Amen Sob

9 Drain Red Info

10 Grass Chin Mill

Answers on page 62

Word Search

The United players can find a team-mate amongst a crowded penalty box, but do you have the same vision? See if you can find the surnames of 10 Reds which are hidden in this wordsearch...

The names to look for are: **Neville** **Hargreaves** **Brown** **Scholes** **Evra** **Rooney** **Smalling** **Fabio** **Gibson** **Nani**

Q	M	R	R	B	D	K	R	N	K	S
S	R	G	R	Z	R	L	I	E	E	Q
V	C	K	N	O	D	N	L	V	Y	Z
R	T	H	O	I	A	W	A	I	F	N
K	V	N	O	N	L	E	R	L	Q	O
L	E	F	T	L	R	L	J	L	X	S
Y	T	R	J	G	E	M	A	E	M	B
A	D	B	R	R	T	S	B	M	N	I
R	N	A	D	M	G	G	Q	R	S	G
V	H	K	G	W	B	R	O	W	N	Y
E	T	R	X	O	I	B	A	F	T	K

Answers on page 62

United Quiz

Q1 Who did Wayne Rooney score his final goal of the 2009/10 season against?

Q2 Paul Scholes scored an injury-time winner against Manchester City last season at Eastlands, but whose cross did he head home?

Q3 What nationality is Federico Macheda?

Q4 Who has made more appearance for United – Rafael or Fabio?

Q5 What shirt number does Antonio Valencia wear?

Q6 In which year did Patrice Evra join United – 2006 or 2007?

Q7 Who scored United's first goal in the 2-1 Carling Cup final win over Aston Villa in February 2010?

Q8 Wayne Rooney was our top scorer in 2009/10 – who was the second highest scorer of the campaign?

Q9 Old Trafford celebrated a special anniversary in February 2010 – what was it?

Q10 What nationality is Nani?

Q11 How many goals did United score against Manchester City last season?

Q12 From which club did Sir Alex Ferguson join United?

Q13 How many Premier League titles has Ryan Giggs won?

Q14 Who scored the team's final goal of the 2009/10 campaign?

Q15 Which Reds midfielder joined United from Tottenham in the summer of 2006?

Q16 Which team did Wes Brown make his Reds debut against in May 1998?

Q17 Bayern Munich knocked United out of the Champions League in 2009/10, but what was the aggregate scoreline?

Q18 Name United's first team coach.

Q19 Paul Scholes scored his 100th Premier League goal for United in March 2010, but who was it against?

Q20 Who is the club's all-time record goalscorer?

Answers on page 62

Who's Going to Score?

Dimitar Berbatov, Ryan Giggs or Federico Macheda are trying to score but only one player can make it through the opposition's defences – can you find out who?

Answers on page 62

60

Win a Signed Football

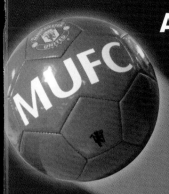

Answer the following question correctly and you could win a United football signed by a first team player.

Q: In what season did United first win the Premier League title?

Send your entry on a postcard by midday on Thursday 31 March 2011 to:

2011 Annual Signed Football Competition
Manchester United Football Club
Sir Matt Busby Way
Old Trafford
Manchester
M16 0RA

(Please include a daytime telephone number)

The first correct entry picked at random will be the winner. The judge's decision is final.

Competition terms and conditions

Entry

1. Manchester United Limited ("Manchester United") is the promoter of the prize draw (the "Prize Draw").
2. Entry to the Prize Draw is on the basis of one entry per person, and in order to enter, participants must correctly answer the question posed and submit their entries by midday on Thursday 31 March 2011 (the "Closing Date")
3. By entering the Prize Draw the participant agrees to be bound by these terms and conditions ("Conditions") and confirms that all information submitted is true, current, accurate and complete.
4. The draw is not open to employees of Manchester United (or its associated companies or subsidiaries), or their families.

Prize

5. The winner will be the first participant chosen at random from all of the eligible entries received on or before the Closing Date.
6. Only the winner shall receive notification from Manchester United. The winner will be notified by telephone as soon as practicable after the Closing Date and by no later than 7 April 2011. Following the draw, the prize will be posted to the winner at the address stated on the entry form. Manchester United is not liable for the acts or omissions of any postal service provider. If Manchester United cannot contact a winner within 24 hours of that winner being drawn (making reasonable efforts), then that winner forfeits the right to any prize and another entrant will be drawn for that prize.
7. The decision of Manchester United is final and no correspondence will be entered into.
8. The prize is a Manchester United football signed by one member of the first team squad. The cost of postage of the prize to the winner shall be borne by Manchester United.
9. The prize is non-transferable and no cash alternative is available. If a winner is unable or unwilling to accept the prize or does not provide the consent requested at Condition 10 below, subsequent draws will take place until a new winner is found who is able/willing to accept the prize and provide the necessary consent.
10. The winners (and their guardians if under 16) will be required to give their consent to the following: (i) for the winners' names to be disclosed to any person requesting that Manchester United confirm the identity of the prize winners; and (ii) for the winners' names and/or photographs to be published for promotional purposes.
11. Subject to Condition 10 above, details of the Prize Draw winners will be made available upon request from Manchester United, Sir Matt Busby Way, Old Trafford, Manchester, M16 0RA (subject to data protection legislation).
12. Manchester United reserves the right to cancel or amend the Prize Draw or these Conditions without notice in the event of the occurrence of circumstances beyond its reasonable control.
13. The Prize Draw, together with these Conditions, is governed by the laws of England and shall be subject to the exclusive jurisdiction of the English Courts.

Quiz Answers

Spot the Difference

Spot the (real) Ball

P57 – True or False

1. TRUE – it's called White Chalk Music.
2. FALSE – he scored a hat-trick on his debut against Fenerbahce.
3. TRUE
4. TRUE
5. TRUE
6. FALSE – John was born on 30 April 1981. whereas Darren was born on 1 February 1984.

P59 – United Quiz

Q1: Bayern Munich
Q2: Patrice Evra
Q3: Italian
Q4: Rafael
Q5: 25
Q6: 2006
Q7: Michael Owen
Q8: Dimitar Berbatov
Q9: The stadium was 100 years old
Q10: Portuguese
Q11: Nine
Q12: Aberdeen
Q13: 11
Q14: Ji-sung Park
Q15: Michael Carrick
Q16: Leeds United
Q17: 4-4 – Bayern went through on away goals
Q18: Rene Meulensteen
Q19: Wolves
Q20: Sir Bobby Charlton with 249 goals

P57 – Anagrams

1. Wayne Rooney
2. Darren Fletcher
3. Ryan Giggs
4. Rafael da Silva
5. Jonny Evans
6. Edwin van der Sar
7. Darron Gibson
8. Ben Amos
9. Rio Ferdinand
10. Chris Smalling

P58 – Wordsearch

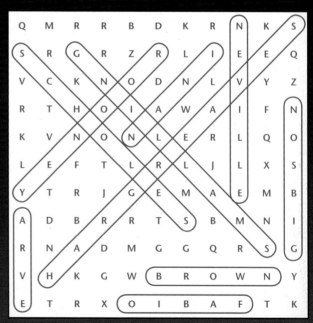

P60 – Who's Going to Score?

Answer: Dimitar Berbatov